An Introduction to Spiritual Therapeutics

Spiritual Psychology in Practice

Robert Sardello

An Introduction to Spiritual Therapeutics
Copyright © 2013 by Author Name.

Book and Cover design Robert Sardello
ISBN: 9781520767345

First Edition: 2017

10 9 8 7 6 5 4 3 2

A note concerning reading this document

This writing is founded in a minimal awakening by the author of the spiritual "I". Thus, the writing consists of a mixture, though quite disciplined, of what is known by the author from 45 years of study and research, and moments of speaking within spirit rather than 'about' it. These moments throw the whole of the text into something other than a set of opinions, or taking up someone else's work (in this case, that of Rudolf Steiner) and synthesizing it in a new way. Such writing is best read by quite deliberately holding disbelief in suspension. Thus, you are not asked to 'believe' anything, just suspend disbelief so that the writing can work. Then, as a secondary movement, certainly evaluate what is said.

Introduction

In this monograph, I explore the possibility of a form of spiritual psychology, a psychology in which body, soul and spirit find true integration. This task of putting forth some sound and clear suggestions for an integrated psychology shall not be easy. In a way, the experience of Wholeness ought to be best guided by religion. But religion, of any sort, can too easily result in a psychology that is 'sectarian', sectarian in the sense that religions try to slant wholeness in one direction, the direction of the approach to faith that each promulgates.

This way of opening a door for the development of a true spiritual psychology does not stand against religion; it stands closer to what can be immediately experienced, if the 'organ' of noticing the fineness of experience is developed.

I do rely, somewhat, on the spiritual science of Rudolf Steiner, without claiming, however, that spiritual psychology is the same as anthroposophical psychology, for as the latter develops, it too has a 'sectarian' slant to it, and risks being the unacknowledged imposition of pre-given concepts onto the project of developing a spiritual psychology.

We must proceed without resorting to the reflections on the 'thought' experience known as theology, or the precepts of any religion, or any given 'spiritual path', and, nevertheless, feel some confidence that if we are indeed true to experience we shall find ourselves in a comfortable relation with both. Standing in the livingness of an imagination of what the human being can become, which is already 'here', ever-present but 'superconscious', that is 'beyond' usual consciousness, and unknown unless specifically developed or awakened, we wish to ask what kind of psychology, what kind of therapeutics, is possible? I believe the answers to this question will indeed be quite astounding.

I have in mind to proceed by following a series of meditations. That is to say, I will not so much be developing an argument nor will I be synthesizing the work of previous scholars and practitioners. Rather I hope to present images that will be possible to enter into and to entertain. This form is somewhat different than what we are used to, though perhaps you will not find it so strange, as you are accustomed to the fact that matters of the soul and of the spirit cannot be approached with the intellect alone.

The process, which we shall follow in this series, may disturb you, for there will be little emphasis on the realm of the visible. I shall report no data, quote no statistics, and cite no experiments or reports. Rather I shall attempt, in as disciplined a manner as possible, to encourage you to hear with your inner, invisible organs, which, in any case, if you are to engage in the work of being help to others in listening to the totality, the wholeness of their inner lives, you must develop the capacity of doing skillfully.

MEDITATION 1 – ON PSYCHOLOGICAL EXPERIENCE

Let us begin with the word *PSYCHOLOGY*. Have you spent time with this word, which names our discipline? The great Phillip Melanchthon, friend of Martin Luther, fellow theologian, introduced the word 'psychology' into the modern vocabulary, inaugurating a new discipline. The word itself - psychology- the logos of the psyche, what does it say? This name says that a language, an original speaking, a logic that is distinctive to the psyche or soul, a 'psychologic' that reveals the life of the soul, constitutes the subject matter of this discipline.

Of great interest, Melanchthon is also the founder of modern economics. Economics seems to have nothing to do with psychology. This word, 'economics', however, means 'the care of the household'. And, if we really had a true soul-psychology, a sacred soul-psychology, a true spiritual psychology, we would be able to coordinate inner life with our 'care of the household' of the world.

Economics, when considered in light of Melanchthon's interest in the psyche, is really the method, when practiced, of the display of all of the psyche within the things and the interrelation of things of the world.

And, perhaps Melanchthon was astute enough to recognize, that without attention to the psyche, what would happen in the world is the 'over-population' of things because 'things' would come to replace the inner life.

He seems to have given us the means to maintain balance between the inner – psyche, and the outer – the 'household'. I doubt that he knew this, but must have known that in formulating economics the way he did, something relevant was being left out, and he gave the 'container' called 'psychology' for this abandoned aspect of the way human beings would come to govern their practical actions in the world. In this exclusion, he also hid the fact that economics is necessarily governed by the psyche. We know this today – we know that everything economic is driven by desire, want, need, vision, and, though economics tries to claim that it is a science, it is driven by the ineffable.

We, of course, have not maintained this balance of 'inner' and 'outer'. Imagine what it would be like if every school of business, everyone seeking, say, a degree in business such as an MBA, would have to have an equal number of courses in spiritual psychology!

Melanchthon did not develop the discipline of psychology, so it did not develop in tandem
with economics, but rather psychology attempted to imitate science, and the work of the word "psychology" was not taken up in a systematic way until Herbart wrote the first textbook of psychology.

Do to the fact that the age of natural science was dawning at the very time Herbart wrote, spelled disaster for this new discipline, which was taken up by the methods of natural science. Natural science has the severe limitation of being able to comprehend only things of the sense perceptible world, and treating things not of the perceptible world as if they were – for example, applying cause-effect thinking to psychological processes; it is a method that must have something to measure. And when this method is applied to those realms that are inherently immeasurable such as the soul, all that results is what William James saw clearly many years ago – one simply finds what one has decided in advance that one would find. So, now, after over one hundred years of this approach to psychology, the result in education is that people enter the study of psychology with a quite good intuition that matters of the soul will be the subject of their studies; the word does not even show up, except a slight nod to Jung and depth psychology. Does anyone enter into the study of psychology who is not, at some level, seeking soul, and are universally disappointed, covering over that disappointment with the need for collective acceptance and the need for employment. What is typically encountered, however, has no connection to anything inwardly recognizable.

It is quite impossible to study psychology without being at the same time that which is studied – if one remains true to the word 'psyche-logos'. And, similarly, it is quite impossible to do psychotherapy without undergoing therapy. Jung astutely pointed out that one can only go as far with a patient as they have gone with themselves. Anyone taking up the tradition of psychotherapy, or any of its derivatives, such as counseling, or even 'spiritual direction', has simply made the choice to spend their life working on their own soul. I am not only suggesting the value of psychotherapists undergoing therapy as part of their professional preparation, but, more importantly, that the doing of psychotherapy always involves the engagement of one's soul and thus all therapy is also self-therapy. Yet, how can one take up this task when the very name of our discipline, which means the care of the soul, the logos, or speech of the soul, is not given attention?

Where can we go to begin to give soul attention? Let us make the task even more difficult by courageously refusing to go outside ourselves, for soul is first of all an experience, and we must inquire into the character of its experience.

In waking life the action of the soul is not directly available to observation. When we look out at the world around us we see the world without recognizing that the soul has an intimate connection with our perception. We would have to have an 'education' into soul life to notice that experience is always a balance between inner experience and outer visibility and action. Modern psychology, as well as modern approaches to spirituality are not very much help here because in psychology, sensing and perceiving are studied with the understanding of the physiological processes involved as central. These processes are indeed involved, but they can never give an account of the actual experience of sensing, for no physiology on its own can ever produce what is most commonplace to us daily – an experience of the world.

The inwardness characteristic of psychology constitutes the modern form of the ancient dictum "Know Thyself." The mode of knowledge of the self, of interior wisdom, follows a different path than the mode of knowledge utilized to understand exterior
things.

Knowledge of external reality is oriented toward understanding the impermanent. But, what we are able to perceive with the senses and convert
into theory, measurement, and prediction, of that, the essence of human reality does not belong. "Know Thyself" means finding inner knowledge of the permanent within the impermanent. The reality of our inner being is not of the same character, not remotely like the sense-perceptible world. And, 'inner' certainly does not mean that the 'outer' is reflected on the 'inside', though, the 'outer' lives within the 'inner' according to the inherent 'laws' of the inner.

In recent times we have learned much from the factual study of the natural sciences and much about the temporal character of human life when the method of the natural sciences is applied to psychology. But the moment the deeper question is asked – where do we come from, and where are we going, and how can these questions be known

in our innermost being – the contributions of external
knowledge are reduced to silence. The external knowledge
of science deserves our greatest respect and admiration. But
in real life this knowledge can take us only to a certain point.

The factual logic that is applicable to the external world falls
short of comprehending the inner
world.

Here, we must follow a different kind of
logic – a psycho-logic. Psychological reality, the logos of the
soul, is a picture-consciousness in which living picture-like
impressions from within 'swim', created every moment by the
soul.

The method of natural science is based on the pretense that
the observer is not part of what is observed, and this pretense
produces valid results to a limited extent. Quantum physics, of
course, does recognize the intertwining of observer and
observed, but that understanding remains abstract, and only
quoted as a cliché by more 'edgy' psychologists. When the
methods of natural science are applied to the soul, the result
is "one-eyed, colorblind" understanding. Psychology cannot
get very far with this pretense because the soul is so
completely merged with the observations it makes, that
pretending the soul is just 'another' 'thing' to be studied,
results not in a genuine discipline, but rather institutionalized
illusion.

In ancient times, knowledge of the soul was not brought
about by detached observation, but by initiation – it was
knowledge by full participation in the mysteries of being. We
must
seek ways to follow this ancient wisdom, but in forms that are
suitable to our present
circumstances. Our first quest will thus be – what is a modern
method of following the ancient wisdom in quest of self-
knowledge?

Soul, in waking experience, is obscured by what is given

through immediate experience of the world around us, namely the visible, tangible, audible, tactile, colorful actuality of the world. We can get a better sense of the soul's action by considering the night dream.

Dreaming is the soul's own production, an example of the spontaneous creativity, its capacity of making felt imaginations of individual spirit, that is always going on, even during waking life. In dream life, soul processes are stronger than the world; thus it can take events of our waking life and weave all sorts of creative fantasy. No dream is simply a repetition of what has happened in waking life, as observation will show. Even the most mundane dream that seems to repeat something from the day will have a creative element in it if looked at carefully. But notice how quickly a dream disappears as soon as we awaken. The soul forces are obscured by the day.

One very intriguing question concerns how the soul forces might be strengthened so that they might become more available for observation
during waking life. Meditation is a process that makes this possible. Meditation concerns learning how to be asleep while remaining awake, and thus rendering the activity of creativity available to consciousness. Sleep itself is a mode of consciousness, as strange as that might initially sound. In addition to waking consciousness and dream consciousness, there is sleep consciousness. Uncovering and exploring this realm of consciousness is of the utmost importance to the development of a psychology of integration. Integration implies something coming together, which was formerly separated.

The task of taking up the ancient wisdom of self-knowledge in new forms involves no less than repairing the split between soul and spirit. The picture-consciousness necessary for self-knowledge has gone underground, available only in the form of dream-consciousness. Dream consciousness is then analyzed by the logic of day-consciousness, but we must find a method for becoming aware of the productions of the soul on their own terms, a method for understanding picture consciousness from within rather than applying analysis to dreams from a perspective outside of their one reality. The first step toward a psychology of integration involves healing the split between soul in its picture-producing capacity and spirit in its knowledge-producing capacity.

The separation between soul and spirit has been a part of human history since the ninth century. At that time, Pope Nicholas declared that spirit does not constitute of reality of human experience.
 Rudolf Steiner, the originator of Anthroposophy, speaks about this in several of his lectures. He was able to come to this knowledge both through historical research, but, more importantly through the capacity of clairvoyance, which he systematically developed, a clairvoyance of the "I", and thus carried out with clarity of consciousness.

Spirit was placed outside, referring to divine beings that could be known only through faith and the teachings of the church. This declaration clarified what was already happening in the evolution of consciousness. The material world was on the way to becoming the basis of all thinking and perception of reality. In former times this was not the case. Spiritual reality was directly 'perceptible'. The outer world was not as we now perceive it – solid, tangible, concrete. The outer world, filled with spiritual presences, was much more like what we now experience as the dream world – shifting, changing, continually in motion, a world clearly alive in all its aspects. By the ninth century this sense of the spiritual character of the world had almost completely disappeared except for those undergoing initiation.

The pyramids and temples of Egypt, the mighty Sphinx, the Egyptian gods, all are testimony to the fact that the world was at one time entirely different than now.
We must not make the mistake of assuming that ancient people were as we are today, living in more primitive circumstances. Reality itself was completely different. The same holds true for the Greek temples, the Greek gods, and

the ritual initiation into the mysteries. The physical world as we now behold it has been with us only since Roman times.

The circumstances leading Pope Nicholas to make his declaration involved a fear that the West was about to be invaded by the East, that the spirituality of the East would overrun the West. And in the East, it is the spiritual world that is primary. The actual, physical world was called 'Maya' or illusion. And, as you know, meditation was and is still the practice, now again coming over to us from the East.

Materialism is far more than a concern for material goods; it is an outlook that says that all processes of the world, of Earth, of the body, and of life can be accounted for on the basis of material processes. So you can see the dilemma we now face. The spiritual world is no longer directly available to experience, and the Eastern path to that experience obliterates the most significant insight of the West, that body and world are not illusions, but central to the divine plan. (It is important to say that Rudolf Steiner found the way through this dilemma, but runs into certain difficulties in bringing those teachings, practices, and actions into the larger world – perhaps because they tend to bypass soul as spiritual 'paths' tend to do.) But the Western way, by itself results in pure materialism. Meditation shall be the key to resolving this dilemma, and psychology shall be the decisive discipline. Let me try to indicate why this is so.

When Nicholas declared the ancient view of human reality as a tripartite unity of body, soul and spirit invalid, soul was also in effect abandoned. Intellect, not in the sense we now know it, but in the more ancient sense of reason, which belongs to activity of spirit, was made into a faculty of the soul. We value intellect so highly because, quite unconsciously, it is value, still given to the activity of spirit within us. Not exactly spirit in a direct way, but more like a reflection of spirit within mind. But the rest of the soul – desire, feeling, appetite, drives, emotions, are in effect left without the inner guidance of spirit, except the guidance of intellect, which is a kind of shadow of spirit within; thus psychology does not presently follow its own inherent logic, but relies on intellectual interpretations and understandings of the activities of the soul.

Only the depth psychology of C. G. Jung departs from this error. The archetypal psychology of James Hillman, who was educated in the psychology of Jung, and knew him well, approached developing the capacity to be simultaneously soul-present and 'world-present', though a specially develop kind of thinking. And, only Rudolf Steiner has developed this capacity to its fullest; he speaks of this capacity as 'living thinking'. But, these vital 'seeds' need much development, much inward development before there can be anything like 'spiritual therapeutics.'

I realize that the words 'spirit' and 'soul' are likely to be confusing. I am very deliberately avoiding presenting a definition of these words, which would be falling into the intellectualistic trap. As we continue with these meditations, however, the quality of the kind of experience we are attempting to address should gradually clarify itself. Soul, we can say at this point, but it is no means a final definition, refers to the inwardness of experience, spontaneously producing itself in the form of images. Without the activity of soul, immediate experience would not exist. The word 'images' here, does not mean anything like 'pictures' that are somehow looked at 'inside'. The specific character of soul-as-image is developed more as we proceed.

Soul, we shall further come to see is distinct from spirit, and is also distinct from mind. Spiritual experience is thus distinct from psychological experience, and psychological experience is different than mental experience. The mind, or the intellect, if you like, I must tell you, does not contain the element of creativity characteristic of soul and it does not contain the element of divine presence characteristic of spirit. "Creative thinking" is a misnomer, because thought in the way the word is ordinarily used, always concerns what we already know. Innovation may be a characteristic of thought but true creativity is not. Concepts are really dead things, thoughts that have already been thought, put cleverly, oh, so cleverly together with logic. I shall say nothing more of intellect at this point, as I am attempting to make a clearing for the utter uniqueness of psychological experience with these various distinctions; in life, of course, body, mind, soul, and spirit function as a unity.

I want to remain steadfast in declaring that the work of psychology is the care of the soul. When a patient comes to me for psychological help, that patient is asking to do soul work. Otherwise there is absolutely no justification for representing myself as a psychologist. If a person comes to me because I am a psychologist aware of the reality and importance of spirit, then that person is longing for something additional, and that additional something is surely not my thoughts about faith or belief or theology or religion, but must be, no matter how vaguely felt, a request for care coming from the integration of spirit and soul inherent in life.

Such a patient does not want religion imposed on psychological problems, which would only serve to repress what the soul is trying to express. Such a 'religious' psychology would be tyrannical. Nor, however, is such a patient requesting that religions be psychologized, (as for example, Richard Rohr excels in doing) that is, reduced to the status of an inner, purely personal image, or an archetype of the psyche. Virtually all of the work in Jungian psychology, for example, that of Jung himself, and more recently the writings of Edward Edinger or Joseph Campbell make this fatal mistake. A psychology incorporating the imagery of religion is very different than a psychology of integration. We must be clear as possible in describing what can be integrated.

Most people believe that they are their bodies and their minds. They do not even know they have souls; they have to be told that by religion, but that telling does not necessarily make soul an actual experience. In fact, it seldom does because what is presented in the telling is usually not from the soul, not itself soul
experience, but rather ideas that have nothing to do with the actual experience of the soul. The soul is that life force,

underlying what we experience of ourselves, others, and the word, an abiding, permanent part of the person, somewhat like an ongoing current, functioning under the guidance of the spirit.

Soul has nothing to do with the personality, which is a composite of all the preferences, ideas, damages, desires, feelings and thoughts that comprise an individual consciousness.
The modern notion of psychology, because it pays no attention to the actual word 'psychology', concentrates on how to become more proficient at being a human personality. The personality is developed to protect the wounds of the soul, to cover them over and to keep oneself from incurring more hurts and pain. The 'persona' is that part of ourselves that is revealed in the world, the aspect we want others to see us as. Psychotherapy for the most part is a kind of analytic of the personality, a vast system for preventing the soul from following its development, and thus also preventing any spiritual growth because spiritual growth can occur only when the voice of the soul is heard. Only the depth psychology of C. G. Jung, and the archetypal psychology of James Hillman avoid this simplification.

Someone, for example, may have a difficulty that he cannot keep a relationship for more than six months and the women in his life are always leaving him. Somewhere along the line he decides if he could improve himself, his ability to relate, then he could have more productive, healthier relationships. He spends years in psychotherapy and thousands of dollars designed to help him with his problem. Years later he is still unable to maintain a relationship with depth. He has developed and improved his personality and perhaps he has grown, but not at the level of the soul. The human ego has grown larger and more cumbersome. He has adjusted further into his damage, covering his fears and hurts with sophisticated words about relationships and more mental junk to wade through. Only the soul can guide and direct one toward change and growth, and does so through the inspiration of the spirit. Yet, psychology, unaware of soul, works with the mental chatter of the personality. We must try to be aware how much our field protects people from change, substituting comfort and success for true soul development.

The most concrete statement I have thus far made about the soul is that it shows itself in the spontaneous production of images; the model for this being the night dream. Now, I must take away what has been given as a kind of place to hold onto. In doing so, I am not being at all abstract; rather, experience is the guide in these matters. You would be misguided if you identified soul with image, for when we think of image we think of a picture being looked at by an observer. Further, to identify soul with image, when image itself has not been adequately described, could easily lead to the impression that a psychology based in soul is the same as dream analysis. The night dream my be the exemplar of soul processes, but analyzing dreams in no way guarantees that the work of psychology is going on. For the most part dream analysis gets caught in applying intellectual systems to dream content – such as symbols, myths, and archetypes. Dream analysis often uses what we 'know' about the collective nature of the soul to interpret what soul produces in the dark of the evening. Soul produces itself in images but the experience of those images is 'from the inside of the images' themselves.

We must not confuse dreaming with going to a movie theatre and looking at a tragic, romantic, epic, or lyric story. In psychotherapy, it is important, not just to ask patients for their dreams, but to hear everything as dream, which means the psychotherapist must have the capacity to hear the inside of everything. And the therapist must develop the capacity to do this without taking the dream qualities apart, look inside, which would not be soul work but rather intellectual curiosity trying to find out what is inside by dismantling it. And, if you dismantle the 'inside', you no longer have an 'inside', it has been made into one more version of the 'outside'.

The art is learning to hear what is inside without taking apart, for taking it apart destroys its character and only reveals more about the analyst than it does the patient. So, image is not a content; it is a way of being present to soul, having as its aim connecting the patient with his or her own soul. The soul, you see, knows exactly what it wants and what it needs from us. It knows how to guide one into healing, and anything done from outside does not produce healing but only gratifies the ego of the therapist as he watches the patient adjust to what the therapist believes is needed.

To learn to hear inside of things requires training in Silence; above all the therapist must learn about Silence, for the image resides in Silence. 'Psyche', the ancient philosopher of soul Heraclitus says, 'loves to hide.' The hiddenness of the soul is not due to defenses; it belongs to the soul's own nature; defenses are its natural protection and are not to be broken down but followed through like a labyrinths. If the protections of soul are respected, soul will show glimpses of itself. I can imagine nothing more tyrannical than accusing a patient of being defensive. How can we expect to be allowed to enter into the soul of another without going through the initiation?

Silence does not mean simply to be quiet and do nothing in therapy, though I think that very often would be the most helpful thing to do. Silence is like resting in the unknown while being fully conscious. To rest in the unknown is difficult indeed, for there, in that holy temple of Silence, our own fears and our own damages cause an inner chatter that is unbearable; and so we tend to speak, not out of the inspiration in the Silence, but out of our own fears and damages. Of course, the therapist would never admit this, and instead uses techniques and words and advise and questions to keep his own fears and damages away by focusing on the patient and the rationalization that he must do something to heal the patient.

A therapy of soul, however, does not find its words in this manner. It does not use dead words, words that screen the unknown, inner fears and damages of the therapist. Nor, however, does soul work use the latest psychological jargon. It does not matter what words are spoken, providing they come out of resting in the Silence.

Utilizing the insights of Gaston Bachelard, I would like to call the language of therapy 'silent speech.' Silent speech is the outward expression of the joy of breathing. One of the meanings of the word 'psyche', is 'breath'. Not the 'breath of spirit', which is 'pneuma', but rather the breath of Life. Our speech is in soul not when it comes out of our thoughts, which are dead things, but out of the holy silence of breathing as-feeling the very presence of Life, not the contents of what we are living – accompanied by presence of heart.

Following Bachelard, 'poetic breath' is a good name for this kind of speech. If you read a poem without a presence to the breath and the rhythm of the heart, it makes no sense at all, for a poem has little information to convey but much soul. The conversations of therapy are not poems, but they are in the imagination of poetry; that is they are creative revelations of the soul. Rather than a knowledge specialist, the therapist is a 'sound chamber', a 'speaking reed.' For a therapy founded in soul, word and breath and heart are one. This is what Gaston Bachelard says about silent speech, word breath:

" We can discover, in the dual breathing of the words 'life' and 'soul', the imaginary theme of 'breathing exercises'. Instead of breathing in,
we will fill our lungs with the word 'life'; 'soul'
is what we will quietly give back to the world. Breathing exercises, far from being the setting in motion of machinery that is watched over by a hygienist, is thus a function of universal life. A day, whose rhythm is marked by the breathing of 'life-soul', 'soul-life', is one that will be in tune with the universe. Between the universe and the breather there is the relationship of the healthy and the healthful. Beautiful breath images vitalize us." (Gaston Bachelard, *Air and Dreams*).

If you pay very close attention to your speaking of the two words 'life' and 'soul' you will learn much about the kind of speech adequate to a therapy based in psyche. In the formation of the word 'soul', the lips, when they are scarcely opened to allow the air to escape, quietly close again. With the word 'life', the exact opposite occurs; then the lips gently separate and seem to take in breath. Practicing this little excises of becoming present to the words 'life' and 'soul' can provide the proper feeling for the work of therapy, an orientation for working in the medium of silent speech. Of course, this is extremely subtle, which is exactly what I wish to emphasize; the work of therapy is art of subtlety. We are so used to running over our patients with our knowledge of dynamics, relationships, analysis, suggestions, tricks, and hypotheses that we can hardly be with them in the subtlety of soul.

Let us consider an instance of soul work, taking a dream as the exemplar of the spontaneous creativity of soul. The dream: in the dream, the dreamer is standing in an open square that has the feeling of an old village. The color and tone of the first part of the dream is that of something old, something out of the past. The dreamer is looking at an old woman, raggedly dressed, extremely sad, in pain. She stands with an infant child. The old woman is sick. She is vomiting, at the same time she is trying to take care of the baby. The baby needs a diaper change. The child is not crying, but looks longingly at the old woman, as if he is trying to help her. The dreamer, who at first is looking at this sad situation, then becomes the child. The dreamer, now the child, has vomit on its hands. The scene shifts. The dreamer is now in a house. He still has vomit on his hands and is running down a hall looking for a bathroom to wash his hands. He comes to a bathroom, but the door is locked; a young woman is inside the bathroom, the dreamer continues down the hall looking for a place to wash.

Our question: how to respect this dream as the manifestation of soul? My interest here is not to provide an example of dream interpretation, and I must emphasize that the approach to this dream is the same as the approach to anything a patient might talk about in the therapy hour; a relationship, a feeling, something that happened at work – all would be approached in the same attitude. The therapist, listening to this dream, must seek to hear it through his own soul. In order to do so, it is necessary to recreate the dream within oneself, to hold the dream as an inner image. This recreation is not an intellectual understanding; it is a grasping of the image – as a whole. That is the important part – to grasp the dream as a whole.

Imagine looking at a painting, in order to see the painting it is necessary to be present to the whole of the painting-, which is a physical, emotional, and spiritual presentation. I cannot see the whole painting of I look at it only as a canvas covered with paint in certain configurations. I cannot see the whole painting if I respond only to the feeling presented before me. I cannot see the whole painting if I only look for the significance of what is presented. The wholeness of the painting must be grasped through the openness of soul. A dream image, a patient's story, an incident told by a patient, a childhood memory told by a patient; all must be first grasped in this total way, held by the capacity to rest in active silence, to relinquish the impulse to do anything with what is presented, realizing that the urge to do so is the attempt to use what is presented by the patient the mind of the therapist. I must be careful not to project my own damage onto the patient, justifying doing so as a system of help.

Now, the dream, in this whole sense is still not within the soul of the therapist if the images are simply taken in and recreated in silence. A second movement of silence is required. The whole picture I now have of the dream, that also must be brought into silence. Ridding oneself of the inner image and holding within the soul only the feeling that is contained within the dream brings that about. To clarify what is meant by producing a picture and then removing it to experience feeling, remember a time when you experienced joy. If you recreate the image of the exact situation of that joy – who you were with, what you were doing, the setting of the occurrence – if you picture this inwardly, then remove the picture and hold within only the feeling of that moment, this gives a clear understanding of what must occur to enter into the soul of an experience presented by a patient in therapy. Out of the silence of this inner feeling, the therapist can speak with assurance that the speech is from the level of the soul.

Return now to the dream image. A Jungian analyst would most likely be immediately aware of the archetypal images of the dream. When I told this dream to one analyst her response was to the old woman in the dream. This analyst said that the old woman is the healer and that the inner healer is sick. This is an intellectual interpretation of the dream, even though it pays
attention and values the dream, in a certain sense, for its own sake. Another analyst might just as well give attention to the child in need; and someone interested in co-dependency would focus on the way the needs of the woman and the child are together in a sick relationship. A similar intellectual interpretation would focus on the dreamer in the dream, saying that the ego is not strong enough to stay in a sick situation, but takes on the mother sickness and runs away to get rid of it. There is something of value in all of these interpretations. But, what is the soul saying through this dream? And how can this be stated without proffering another intellectual interpretation?

The therapist must first re-create the image of the dream as a whole within the imagination, which is far more than having thoughts about the dream. This act of re-creation, which I have called an action of imagination, here means simply that the dream picture is recreated; strictly speaking, such a re-creation is not an action of imagination but of memory, and this is quite objective. However, memory of this sort is always creative, it is not 'logical' memory, but whole memory, the 'place' where memory meets psyche. The therapist must nevertheless undergo the discipline of learning to do this without
allowing one's own fancy to enter. Once the dream as a whole has been grasped, imagination proper then enters.

I do not mean that the therapist 'makes up' something to say about the dream; rather, the imagination works with the static memory image to bring it alive within oneself, relating every part of the dream to every other part. To return, then, to the dream: when an old setting appears, an old situation from the past, an old woman sickness comes up for the dreamer, the dreamer becomes a child in need of care. The child becomes unaware of his need for care when the old woman sickness appears. The child-dreamer focuses on the old woman sickness that he feels is on his hands. The child-dreamer seeks to rid himself of the sickness he feels is on his hands by looking for a cleansing place, which is closed to him and occupied by a young woman. The young woman locks him out of cleansing the old woman sickness that has come up on him again. The dreamer continues to look for a place to cleanse the sickness he feels is on his hands but which is not his sickness.

I do not suggest that the therapist speak in this way to the patient about the dream. What is important is that the therapist has developed the capacity to take in the dream as a whole. When felt within the depth of soul, held carefully, and experienced in this way, it is out of this active silence that something of therapeutic value can be said. In fact, I would suggest that
anything that is said out of this creative silence in which the soul of the patient and therapist have been united into one will be of therapeutic value, because it come from the level of soul in which what is objective – the patient's dream, and what is subjective, the therapist's imagination have united into a single reality.

I have utilized the instance of the dream to promote a feeling of what it is like to engage in a therapy of the soul. (The word 'therapy', comes from the imagination, in Greek times, of the 'Therapeutes', which are the 'spirits of attending soul. If we can feel into the depth of this word, what is encountered in the depths of Silence are the 'Therapeutes', and it they who are the mediums of 'therapy'). None of what has been said can be made into a new system of analysis without destroying the intention of this example; it is not a new technique. The life of the soul cannot be explained out of a web of thoughts separated from the soul. To understand soul it is necessary to enter into the creative and active powers of the soul. We must learn to release standing outside of things in order to think about them and learn to think within them. Everything that is arbitrary, thought up, falls away.

What we are not accustomed to, because we live in a scientific civilization which certainly

pervades all of psychology, is to proceed in soul work according to the laws of the soul itself. The first and most important of these laws, the psycho-logic, the logic of the psyche, is that the soul's spontaneous creativity goes from the Whole, which is archetypal in character into the particular given experience, and the particular is an intensification of the Whole. When a person really grasps the Whole then he can grasp the particulars; proceeding in this attitude we follow the soul itself, doing the same thing the soul is doing when she lets creations go forth out of the mysterious Whole. As long as a person does not feel the working and creating of soul, his thinking remains separated from the patient. As soon as he feels how the soul lives and is active within his own inner life, he looks upon himself and his patient as one Whole; what appears as something subjective in his inner life has objective validity as well; the subjective becomes objective.

The development of a mode of consciousness capable of simultaneous participation in and knowledge of the reality of soul, is, I believe, the prerequisite to a spiritual psychology and to the practice of a spiritual therapeutics. It is a primary way of avoiding theorizing, and the mental application of that theorizing. In order to work toward a psychology of integration of this sort, we must learn to work with an atmosphere that can truly further this quest. We must become aware of our connections with ancient wisdom and take up the wisdom of tradition in ways suitable to the present world. With all our knowledge of the external world, we are further today from the truth of the divine world than were the

with their knowledge derived from the mysteries. But
ack must be found again. We must return to the old
╌╌ with new forms. We are now living at the close of an
epoch in which the psychological has been split from the
spiritual, to the detriment of both. We must seek the forms of
consciousness that can encompass both and that can lead
to a new understanding of human reality.

Psychology has a decisive part to play in the development of
the capacity of living and working as fully integrated persons
rather than as narrow specialists, but only if psychology itself
can free itself from its specialist mentality. The development of
a picture-consciousness in the full light of waking life is where
we must begin. The next step, which we shall consider in what
is to follow, concerns, within this new form of picture-
consciousness, the development of an understanding of spirit,
not as faith or as belief, but in terms of its own forms of
experience.

MEDITATION 2 – ON SPIRIT

In this mediation I wish to consider some of the ways spirit is an
actual experience of daily life and the manner in which
learning to give attention to spirit has a decisive effect in the
practice of psychotherapy, the beginning of an alteration
into spiritual therapeutics. Even more than in the mediation on
soul and psychology, we must hold in abeyance any thoughts
concerning spirit that would come from the reflections of
religion or of theology, feeling some assurance that if we can
remain true to experience, we shall later discover a healthy
relationship between the psychology of soul and spirit and
religions traditions, should that be an interest.

I have had to ask myself how spirit shows up in
psychotherapy. This question must be pursued without
imposing any already formulated spirituality or theology on

the situation of psychotherapy. To begin to understand the way spirit is to be found, look at what actually happens in therapy that takes place through the word. I am excluding from consideration all body therapies because I have no experience with them; as well, I am excluding family systems therapies and other group therapies. The model I wish to look to is individual
psychotherapy. In that situation, the medium is speech, talking with one another, patient and therapist. Other modes of therapies, though, can also be considered through the activity of the word, for ' as 'word'is not confined to the verbal.

What is talked about? What the patient dreams; what the patient does; what the patient feels; what the patient thinks. The content varies considerably, but dreams, feelings, thoughts, actions are the arena – when experienced from within. We have already reflected on dreams, not as content, but as the exemplar of the creative activity of the soul. Now, staying very descriptive, we must pay attention to the immediately given fact that the person embodies – these dreams, feeling, thoughts, and actions, which are spoken, are spoken by some-body; they are never abstract. Further, this person, with body, who speaks these things, does so by means of the breath, for speaking is a matter of breath, or a certain modulation of breathing. In all older languages, the words used to designate the element of air bound up with breathing, or the act of breathing, served at the same time to express the relationship of man to the Divine, or even the Divine itself. One need think only of the words **Brahma**, and **Atma** of the ancient Indians, the **pneuma** of the Greeks, the **spiritus of the** Romans. The Hebrews expressed the same idea when they say that

Jehovah had breathed the breath of life into man and that man in this way, and the **Spiritus** of
The Romans. So, here we begin to hear the word 'breath' in a different manner than was developed earlier in this writing. A most
interesting question – what is the difference in experience of

this one word, which are two subtle realities?

What lies behind all these words signifying 'spirit' is the feeling familiar to man in those times, that breathing was not only a means to keeping the body alive, but that a spiritual essence streamed in with the breath. So long as this condition prevailed, people could expect that by changing their manner of breathing they had a means of bringing the soul into stronger relationship with spiritual Powers, as was attempted in Eastern Yoga.

Two things are of interest in recognizing the connection between breath and spirit. First, I am not suggestion that the way to connect with spirit is through the breathing techniques of Eastern meditation. Many people these days are drawn back to such practices because there is indeed a relationship between breath and spirit. These approaches, however, completely forget that the very nature of the appearance of spirit has changed. These approaches do not realize the full significance of the fact that the
appearance of 'spirit' has changed – it is not a matter of breathing sensory experience in and out. As, at one time, concentration on the breath, on breathing, took one into spirit-experience, now, concentration on the breathing in and breathing out of the world that takes place in sensing is required – not on the content of what one senses, but on the 'sensory' breathing itself. Consider this deeply, for it is exactly what goes on in therapy, though it not something any 'psychological theory' is aware of. Think of that – spirit, breath, embodied, individualized, then, is the spirit, breath presence, of soul-spirit.

In former times, to make connection with spirit it was necessary to go out of the body. Now, because of increasing 'density' of incarnation, it is necessary to find spirit by going into body, not in the really ignorant ways of body therapies, but into body through the word – and the word became flesh. The word belongs simultaneously to the body and to the breath. I am not deriving this way of looking at the situation from theology. Without the sense of body-soul-spirit as Word, we retain a materialistic outlook on the world, and therapy is unwittingly a companion of the outlook of materialism, helping the person in pain to become a better materialist.

I cannot look at the patient sitting by me as a mass of physiology and at the same time see an

individual soul and spirit. Integration begins with the capacity to experience the unity of body, soul, and spirit.

The body, from this viewpoint of unity, consists of far more than what we are accustomed to thinking of as the physical body. The physical body belongs to the mineral world and does obey the laws of the physical world. But that body is not the sensing, feeling, acting, thinking body. No combination of material elements can ever produce the living body. Nevertheless, we share the physical body with the mineral world. Completely interpenetrating the physical body is what could be called the 'life body'. The 'life body', strictly speaking, is not another body, but refers to the life forces within the body, the forces of growth. This body, we share with the plant world. I am not speaking of plants as botanist does, for this discipline, since the time of Linnaeus has been concerned only with the naming and classification of plants and their parts. There was once another approach to botany, called vitalism, which understood that plant life could not be understood by mechanical principles. But this approach, which recognized something of the mystery of plants, was very unclear about what comprised the life force of plants – they simply called it a vital principle. I am proceeding much more descriptively; we see plant life grow, and that is something that the human body shares with the plant world. The
mineral body, per se, does not grow. Ancient spiritual traditions that were aware of the living forces of growth of the human body called this body the etheric body. (This way of thinking characterizes, in the tiniest way imaginable, how Rudolf Steiner proceeds in the development of the Wisdom of the Human Being.)

Now, all of this may seem very far removed from spirit; let me assure you, it is right to the point, but we will have to follow this descriptive approach to the human body through its complexity in order to understand what is meant by spirit. As a psychologist, and as a 'noticer' of soul and spirit, I must stay within the realm of what is immediately given rather than approaching spirit through faith in the attempt to develop a psychology that is congruent with faith. In order to bridge the tremendous gap between psychology and faith, it is necessary to have a view of human reality in its wholeness. Such a view avoids the mechanism of behaviorism and so-called scientific psychology, which understand the human body only as the mineral level where mechanical causation does function.

"Mechanistic' psychology attempts to apply laws of mechanical causation, appropriate to the mineral level of the body to levels of human action that have nothing to do with mechanical causation. For example, it is quite possible to understand the movement of the bones of the body through mechanical causation; the muscles cause the movement of the bones through this kind of cause. But it is not possible to understand the movement of the muscles through the principles of mechanical causation. Through an act of will the muscles come into action. That is a fact available to immediate experience; all one needs to do is to wiggle the big toe. There is absolutely no evidence that a motor nerve impulse is sent form the brain down to the big toe, for the 'wiggling' is experienced right there at the site of its occurrence. Well, if we really stay close to experience, we are forced to admit that something immaterial is going on right within the materiality of the body, that spirit is not at all divided from the human body.

I am not equating the will with the growth forces of the body; we still have to arrive at how the will is within the body; but we would never be able to do so with a mere mechanical conception of the body. All talk of will or of spirit, if we understand the body purely in terms of the mechanistic imagination, is nothing but abstraction. And when will or spirit is talked about in this abstract way nothing can come of it that is helpful to the soul, for no connection is made to the soul. Talking of will or spirit abstractly can only have the effect of exercising intellectual power over another.

In addition to the physical body, our share in the mineral world, and the body of growth forces, our share in the plant world, there is the sensate body, the body that experiences pain and pleasure. Here we recognize a form of consciousness, and thus it is possible to say that the sentient body is at the same time the sentient soul, because we are describing a form of inner experiences. When we say, "That is a nice, pleasant color", this is an activity of the soul, of the sentient soul. But, notice, we have not abstracted this activity from the body. The sentient body is the bearer of consciousness, the mode of consciousness that is characterized by two qualities -- sympathy and antipathy. Thus, at this level of consciousness we experience emotions, which are polar in nature – pain and pleasure. When this level of consciousness interpenetrates the forces of the growth body, we experience the sensations of physical pain or physical pleasure.

You have all had occasions, I am sure, of sitting down with a patient who begins a session by saying that they are in pain. And I am sure that you have all experienced this kind of pain yourselves. It is quite an extraordinary experience, because it is real pain and it is felt in the body, but it is not physical pain. If this kind of pain persists, physical symptoms do develop because this emotional pain is so close to the growth forces of the body, even though this is a
pain of the soul. Besides sympathy and antipathy, the sentient soul is characterized by yet another experience, that of desire. Desire also has, however, the character of sympathy and antipathy, though here both movement towards and movement away are much more combined. Thus, a person caught in desire can be in dire pain or in pleasure, or a mixture of both together.

Finally, dream consciousness also characterizes the sentient soul. Dream consciousness, we have already seen, is the exemplar of the activity of soul because this activity is the first level of soul. Jungian psychology tends to make this activity the whole of the psyche, though Jung himself did not because he recognized and thoroughly explored a phenomenology of the self, which involved him in the realm of spirit. But what we have said of the sentient soul thus far also applies to dreams. Dreams are sometimes very involved in the body, so that often body sensations accompany dreams, or waking from a dream in a sweat, or experiencing intense feelings in dreams. But dreams can also appear that seem relatively independent of the physical body. So we have a sense of the soul being a middle ground - between the body and what we are about to describe, self.

These days there is quite a lot of lofty talk about 'the self'. But we shall stay small and descriptive. I wish to begin by referring to that small, mighty moment when the child transforms from a crawling creature into a standing being, a bodily transformation of great significance. And with this event comes that momentous occasion when each of us has said of ourselves "I". This 'I' is completely unique, and applies only to ourselves. We call no one else "I". In this transformation of the body from crawling to standing and the naming of ourselves within as "I" has no counter part anywhere in the world; it is a pure experience of the inner spirit, and has nothing to do at this point with egotism. Egotism, to which we are all subject, occurs when the 'I' is immersed in the world and we seek our satisfactions there rather than the purpose of the 'I' which is to make connection with the soul and seek the spiritual development of the 'I' through the mediation of the soul. The disconnection of the 'I' from the soul produces all of the illusions of life that make impossible any inner peace. The extent of this absence of connection is really quite hard to imagine, for perhaps thousands of years now this splitting of the 'I' from the soul has been perpetuated by all of the institutions of civilizations – institutions such as economics, education, marriage, religion, science, technology, commerce, politics, medicine.

No malice is intended by pointing out that the world does not support the deployment of the soul. For the past thousand or so years, the individual spirit has been occupied in the development of the world. Now, however, we are at a crisis of great proportions due to the neglect of soul. The world had seen progress, but not development, a term I wish to reserve for the destiny of the soul. This crisis, which is quite apparent every where – the present breakdown of all of the institutions mentioned, and more, presents a very great opportunity for an integrated psychology; herein lies the possibility of making an active contribution to re-establish connection to the soul, helping culture find its true purpose.

This very large project which I propose is the purpose of psychology at the present time, and can only take place by means of psychology of integration, by spiritual psychology, obviously, will not be welcomed by the world. Most people who enter psychotherapy hope to strengthen the forces of egotism in order to fit in comfortably with the world and do not have an inkling of what soul is all about, or feel that is taken care of by the church. In order to understand this situation from the viewpoint of a psychology of integration, we must look at the psychology of egotism as a deviation, a necessary pathology of the spirit.

In order to understand egotism, we must understand the duality of the 'I'. This duality is present in the very character of the letter 'I'. This letter stands, reaching from the ground to the sky, an upright letter like the child who has just learned to stand on his own. The bottom of this letter 'I' we can picture as the ego drawn to, interested in, involved with the world in order to gratify itself. This is the ego of egotism, which becomes dependent on the world and others for its own definition. This is the ego disconnected from the soul and thus lost, searching about to gain power for itself; power in the form of control over others, positive of things, wanting comfort. The top of this letter 'I' is the ego as spirit, enveloped by soul-forces, united with the body in order to go through a series of developmental phrases, impelled by an inner drive

□

expand into the spiritual world after having enriched itself with experiences of life on earth.

Both senses of "I" are needed for integration. When the people of the world live only the "I" that is world involved, the gathering of more and more 'things', sometimes physical, sometimes emotional, sometimes intellectual – then it begins to seem that there is only the outer world, 'thing-afied'. Inwardly, what is there – only unconscious guilt and its attendant activity
of self-destruction – self here as the egotistic- I. We see this movement of guilt and self-destruction going rampant in the world at this time.

There is much interest at the present time in the 'higher-ego', spoken of as the 'higher-self'. The so-called New Age movement concentrates on various techniques to achieve the experience of the 'higher-self'. I call this movement the 'enlightenment club'. People spend large amounts of money attending weekend seminars to find ways to leave their bodies. If egotism constitutes a disconnection with soul, explorations of the 'higher-self' constitute a schizophrenic split. Yet, this movement, which is just beginning and will increase in strength, indicates a real yearning for spirit. There is much valuable information to be found in the various techniques of the New Age movement. At the same time, there exists the strong likelihood that this movement will produce a new a new kind of greed, -- workshops, seminars, devices of every sort, all claiming to have, for a few hundred dollars, the key to spiritual experience. And, thus, this kind of 'spirit-movement falls into the 'thinga-fication' of the world, and becomes another factor of self-destruction.

While we have to contend now with the given way of naming the presence of spirit in the development of the individual as the 'higher
ego', this naming needs to be filled in with a description of the particular kind of experience what characterizes it. Because, in everyday life, this ego is indeed intimately linked with the more ordinary sense of ego that finds such strong

worldly support, it takes a particular discipline to come to a sense of the spirit. This discipline involves entering into a new experience of the inner life of thought. The task of the individual spirit is to bring about the necessary transformations of body and soul that bring about a harmony between body, soul, and spirit in relation to the particular earthly activities each of us find ourselves within. I shall, later, describe the exact nature of this transformative work and relate it to the arena of psychotherapy. But the spirit must be free to do this transformative work; thus, it is imperative to give voice to the actual experience of spirit.

In former times, the experience of spirit was brought about through the process of spiritual initiation. The mystery religions of ancient Persia, Egypt, Greece, the Celts, the Norse, the American Indians, and the Oriental practices, all had the aim of guiding the initiate into the experience of living spirit. To attempt to return to ancient practices of initiation, because such a return negates history, produces spiritual experiences that cannot connect with the actuality of the world. Such experiences are fine,
and can perhaps ameliorate the stress of life, but
that is something of a palliative rather than experiencing life itself, within the complexity that we now live, the capacity of spirit-presence.

Religion too fails in its task when it steps beyond the bounds of being a guide and seems to offer ready-made answers. Rather than fostering individual transformation it become a drug, a form of addiction, a cultural co-dependency in which the weak rely on the power of the church for a weekly injection of spirit with which one goes forth to try and inject into others. While this is indeed a characterization of religion and not religion per se, it is what happens to the expression of religion that is still absent of the presence of the human being as integrated body, soul, and spirit. Religion still takes itself as the arbiter of what counts as 'spirit', dolling it out in ritual, sermon, and teaching, as if it belonged to the holders of religion but not inherently to everyone else.

☐

I want to follow this aside from the meditation in which we are engaged to its conclusion, knowing that the darker side of religion is difficult to face. But, since I have opened it up, we must try to see it clearly. Then we will return to a description of the experience of the 'higher ego'.

I shall follow through the difficulty of religion

becoming a powerful drug, by describing an instance that I am actually familiar with that shows how an individual can try to solve their own problems by entering an institution that solves other people's problems. When religion gets off the track of its true purpose, I believe the process through which this deviation takes place is similar to what I am about to describe. This process is not exclusive to religion; this description concerns more the healing profession, but I think you will be able to readily apply it to what can happen in the confusions of religion.

I am thinking of a patient who has recently entered psychotherapy. He is a lawyer by profession. He is the victim of very severe emotional child abuse. He is a criminal lawyer, works alone, and has a very unsuccessful practice. He entered therapy because of difficulties he was experiencing in relationship with a woman. He feels he can never be good enough for her, that he can never meet her standards. Once, when he broke a very minor promise made to her, he felt that he had committed the worst sin imaginable. He went to church and prayed with the thought that perhaps this 'sin' would take him to the very bottom, that at last he had sunk so low that he could not possibly do anything worse. I asked him what he really wanted in life, hoping that he could enter into his feelings. Instead, he said that what he most wanted to do was to leave his profession as a lawyer, go through training as an abuse counselor, become the head of an abuse clinic, be a leader in that clinic that would set standards for all those who worked there, get himself into a power position in which he could set the standards for the state and then for the nation. Then he said, he also considered doing this on an international scale, but was a little concerned that this might not happen. But, if we look at the process we see that here is a person, severely abused, planning, with the best of intentions, to institutionalize his own abuse, where it could be legitimately passed on to others. And there is great energy in him to do just this. My question is simply how often does this process occur in those who train for the ministry?

The ego is much misunderstood in psychology, either elevated to the central position of authority in the personality or maligned as the usurper of the total field of psychological experience. In either attempt to emphasize the ego, an adequate description of the actual experience of what is popularly called the 'higher ego' is decidedly lacking. If we return to the letter 'I', attempting to get a real feeling of this letter, we notice that the 'I' is not singular,
But a polar unity – the lower "I" concerned with

consciousness of the world; the higher 'I' concerned with transformation of this consciousness of the world into soul consciousness oriented toward Wholeness as an actual reality, experienced. The world is the setting in which we are now given the task of making connection with our soul in this way. The body is the medium through which the world becomes an experience of soul; and the soul is the middle ground between body and spirit, and once sensing spirit, a turn-around occurs wherein soul becomes devoted in attention to the reality of spirit, here, not some vague 'elsewhere'. The 'I', which is both our individual experience of ourselves, our body, and the world as well as the capacity to enter into the spiritual significance of these experiences, thus functions both as an aspect of the world and is also not of this world. To understand this polar function of the 'I', we must describe the relation of the 'I' to the body on the one hand and the relation of the 'I' to the realm of spiritual experience on the other.

First, it is obvious that the 'I' constitutes self-consciousness, unique to human beings. No other creature can be characterized by self-consciousness, which is different than

consciousness-of-self. And, because we are avoiding all varieties of dualism, we must
describe how this self-consciousness is embedded, as it were, with body.

The body consists of three independent yet interrelated systems, which can be described in a general way as the brain-nerve system, the heart, lung, blood, or circulatory system, and the metabolic system. There is also of course, the skeletal system, but we can consider the skeleton as the framework, the physical upholder of the body. The bones are, on the one hand, the dead part of us, and at the same time, deep within the bones, in the marrow, life-sustaining blood is created.

The three body systems, brain-nerve, the circulatory or rhythmic system, and the metabolic system, are concentrated respectively in the region of the head, the region of the heart, and the region of the stomach. The three systems are certainly present throughout the body, but have their focus in these three areas. These three systems correspond to three modes of self-consciousness, the nerve-brain system corresponds to thinking; the rhythmic system corresponds to feeling; and the metabolic system corresponds to willing. It is as if we are a 'holy trinity', three in one, one in three.

Because the soul is embodied, these organ systems are at the same time regions of experience, a fact that anatomy or physiology is incapable of understanding, or understood in a confused way because of their materialistic bias. The bodily 'I' is actually a polarity, with willing functioning at the life pole and thinking functioning at the consciousness pole, with feeling providing the flow between the life processes and the thought processes. In this way of describing self-consciousness, will is the most surprising. We are accustomed to thinking of will as belonging to the realm of thought combined with desire – I think about something and feel an impulse to act --but will is actually in our metabolism, that is, it is the 'grounding' of I-as-spirit.

To assure ourselves of the truth concerning the interaction of our I with will and body, we need not wait until an adequate method has been developed by outer scientific research. We may turn to direct self-observation as a valid means of investigation. Take a position close to a smooth wall, so that one arm and hand, which are left hanging down alongside the body, are pressed over their entire length between body and wall. Try now to move the arm upward, pressing it against the wall as if you wanted to shift the latter. Apply all possible effort to this attempt, and maintain the effort for about one minute, then step away quickly form the wall by more than the length of the arm, while keeping the arm hanging down by the side of the body in a state of complete relaxation, the arm will be
found rising by itself. The self-consciousness of will makes will seem to be within thought, but the operation of the will is in the metabolic system.

The description of self-consciousness as the totality – thinking, feeling, willing, needs to be furthered one more step, for we must also characterize the manner in which the soul is involved in this wholeness if we are to remain true to an integration of body, soul, and spirit. Corresponding to brain-nerve system and to thinking, there is the soul experience of memory. Corresponding to rhythmic system and to feeling, there is the soul experience of dreaming. Corresponding to metabolic system and to willing, there is the soul experience of fantasy. Fantasy, as we shall see later is quite different than imagination.

Now, let us look a bit more closely at what has been just presented, for most of what psychotherapy currently takes as its field can be understood within what I have just described; and you can see just how limited psychotherapy is because, we have yet to describe the whole region of true transformation, which is connected, not with the lower ego or the world ego, but with the higher ego or what I would like to speak of as true spirit. By remaining true to the totality of human experience, there are some new ways to look at

☐

psychotherapy.

First, let us call this kind of psychotherapy based in the description of human experience of the ego, world based psychotherapy to distinguish it from psychotherapy that consciously takes the higher sense of spirit into account. This kind of psychotherapy has much to offer, but it is not yet a therapy based on a true psychology of integration. We still have to arrive at what a therapy based in true integration might look like. Accepting the challenge of integration involves no less than re-visioning psychology in a manner that makes possible a natural rather than a forced connection to the truths of the reality of spirit-as-lived. Such a re-visioning of psychology will take years of concentrated effort and dedication, and might proceed more easily were it called 'spiritual therapeutics', for then, much of the illusions of psychology might be sidestepped.

If psychotherapy were based upon the description of human experience thus far provided, it would be limited to adjustment and could not have transformation as an aspect of its realm of concern. Such a psychology, while full and rich, would still be worlds apart from integrated spirit experience. It could, however, be a very effective and necessary work of helping to bring into harmony the realms of thinking, feeling, and willing. If these modes of experience are out of alignment, it is impossible
for the soul to carry out its development. When thinking, feeling, and willing are not acting in harmony there is a basic imbalance and the life of spirit is not free to do its work of transforming soul because it is not free; spirit, in such instances spends itself, as it were, on functioning in an imbalanced way. Let me provide an image from psychotherapy of such imbalance.

The patient is an artist, a very accomplished artist who has in recent years come upon rather widespread recognition. His painting is of an abstract nature, but quite different than most contemporary abstract painting. Art critics have said the following about his work: some technical details – he stretches paper over wood frames and coats with graphite and wax; the mixture of graphite and wax can cause the black undercoating to become almost a reflective surface, while at the same time it is an absorbing absence; some influences – critics locate his painting within the modernist tradition, liken it to that of Mark Rothko, with an infusion of Oriental aesthetics; what his paintings represent – it is a return of spiritual reality to art. His paintings are objects of contemplation rather than objects of perception; to see them, one must enter into spirit or soul.

I start with this description of his art because this person is very spiritual in one sense, as can be

seen from his art. But his art is way ahead of his experience of himself. He is very mental, on the one hand, and very willful on the other. The willfulness shows as strong aggression that is constantly held in check by his thoughts, but pours out every so often in angry frustration. In his earlier years, running was an outlet for these strong forces of his body, but a knee injury has made it impossible for him to continue this way of releasing the metabolic forces of will. Because spiritual forces are very strong in him, he is both a very gentle and kind person, while a seething volcano rages within his body. In addition, while he has worked very hard for many years on his spiritual development, it remains at a level of mental understanding. His warmth and kindness can pass for genuine feeling, but it is dry kind of feeling. He also experiences chronic physical symptoms in the region of the rhythmic system; a constant sinus condition that makes breathing somewhat difficult; a feeling of dryness in his lungs that makes his voice raspy; and a high cholesterol level of the blood. These symptoms all indicate that he is blocked in his feeling. A recent dream shows the soul's way of characterizing what is going on. In the dream, he is in a city, near buildings that are falling apart in ruins. He is standing with another man. As they stand amidst the ruins, broken glass begin to fall on the head of the dreamer. The man next to him directs the dreamer to cover his head; the dreamer does so, putting on a cap.

Concerning the dream; briefly, the dreamer stands in the midst of a physical falling apart, while crystallized light falls on his head and he is directed to place something soft between his head and the material falling from the sky. We gain the feeling from the dream that the spiritual light entering the dreamer is presently dangerous because it is brittle, and that he needs to soften his connection with the spiritual world; the physical ruins of the building may be like his own body falling apart. We could say, then, that there is an imbalance here, with thought and will being out of harmony with feeling. The feeling life must be strengthened. The feeling is also present that a strengthening of the feeling life will lead to transformation of the spiritual life that he has worked too hard to find, but cannot take place as long as there is this imbalance. Dream-work, because it can make conscious the soul's experience of the rhythmic system of the body will prove to be valuable for this person. Without the understanding of the connection between the rhythmic system, feelings, and dreams, any attempt to foster the feelings of this person, a, would most likely not only prove ineffective, but more importantly, would destroy the most important spiritual orientation of this person.

As long a psychology fails to recognize the reality of spirit as a mode of experience, the experience of the infusion of the divine into human in the utter uniqueness of our individuality, an integrated psychology cannot be brought about. Spiritual concerns can only be added on from the outside as matters of faith and belief supported by enthusiasm but lacking the force to touch the person in a deep and lasting way unless connection is made with the ineffable of experience. Such experience cannot be measured, calculated, or known by any external means. On the other hand, when connection is made to the spirit as it manifests in the full individuality of the higher-ego, the self, then matters of faith and belief light up from within.

Psychology can easily turn into an institutionalized power trip, as can religion, when there is an absence of the truth that all power is divine power. Approached through the lower-ego alone, psychology's venture into spiritual realms can lead only to attempts to have control over divine power. The task of our time is to learn to allow divine power to work through us, to transform our life and transform the world. The need for control keeps us locked in the ego of egotism, seeking our own comfort and satisfaction rather than following the path of the soul.

One of the great illusions of psychology is that it can lead to inner peace and satisfaction. Such an understanding of psychology is actually based on the assumption of materialism, from which we derive our notions of satisfaction. The psychology of self-satisfaction is founded in what we think we want, which is conditioned by what the world currently presents as most appealing – comfort. The psychology of integration follows another premise – it seeks to find what the soul wants and the courage to follow the path the soul presents to us.

The quest for a psychology of integration follows two directions at the same time. It looks upon the person and the person's relation to others and to the world, the engagement in worldly concerns as a good. If the world and others would not be seen as a good, then we would not be concerned with psychology but with mysticism, with how to get out of the world to seek union with the divine. At the same time the psychology of integration sees worldly engagement as good, it sees the infusion of the soul with the desire for a higher good, the impulse to utilize our worldly concerns in service to the development of a higher spiritual sense. Such a psychology is not dualistic because it recognizes the inherent polarity of the ego that we belong both to the world and to the spirit at the same time. Logic cannot comprehend this polarity; psycho-logic can.

We have now looked at two large dimensions that are the foundation of a psychology of integration, spiritual psychology – an entrance into the gates of ancient wisdom in which the soul's own mode of presenting itself can breathe again in the modern world, and an understanding of the nature of spirit as the duality of world participation and reception of divine power. These two foundations allow us to now go further into the dimensions of an integrated psychology and how it might operate in the realm of psychotherapy. Hopefully, much of the power inherent in current psychology has been dissolved and we are more ready to ask how psychology can be a guide rather than a regulator of the soul's action in the world. We shall address this concern in the next meditation.

MEDITATION 3 – ON TRANSFORMATION

We now want to look at the field of psychology and psychotherapy from the viewpoint of the higher-ego, the 'I' that is not the worldly immersed 'I' but the 'I' in the aspect of what Jung called the Self. But, there is much confusion concerning the self, particularly between a sense of spirit coming from the East and the Western sense of spirit. Jung himself became more Eastern when working with spirit, even in his understanding of rituals such as the Mass. There is much to be learned from the East concerning spirit, but the particular task of the West must be understood in order to produce a fruitful dialogue rather than the absorption of one by the other. In order to avoid this confusion which is inevitable if the stance taken is that spirit must be added to psychology, we must have an informed feeling of the cultural situation of the West in regard to spirit. Then, the specific manner in which the higher-ego can come into relation with psychology can be developed as the completion of the view of the human experience thus far presented.

The Grail legend, particularly the epic, Parsifal, by Wolfram von Eschenbach, which was written
In the tenth century, is actually a central archetypal story in image form, of the quest for
spirit in the West. The keeper of the Grail castle is incurably wounded. The significance of this wound is that it is a loss of spirit and a loss of wholeness, through a concentration on using the forces of desire for self-interest. It is the task of Parsifal, through the trials he must undergo in quest of the Holy Grail, to heal the Grail King. The secret code to this story, what is required to bring about wholeness, is sacrifice. That is what Parsifal must do over and over again in his ventures. The task requires much more than being a good person, for Parsifal is a very good person, ideally so. The task requires much more than being a heroic person, for Parsifal is heroic from the beginning and does not have to learn this virtue. And the particular nature of sacrifice is given through the images of the story; Parsifal must learn to love. Sacrifice is synonymous with love. He must learn to love soul through giving without recompense from others. In the East, through meditative practices, connection with divine spirit is enacted. In the West, the task is to find spirit while remaining dedicated to the tasks of the world. It is not found by going off to Ashrams, temples, and initiation centers, but by learning to serve others in the world.

A psychology of integration, I believe, must have at its heart the capacity to awaken this process of transformation from a concern for oneself to a concern for others, without diminishing the
lower-ego in the process. For the task of the West is to develop spirit in full consciousness and full individual freedom, while for the East, it has been to find spirit by diminishing ego consciousness and relinquishing freedom. A psychology of

integration requires great strength and great wisdom, for it is out of strength and wisdom that love will emerge.

The Grail story is actually more complex than the quest for spirit; it is the quest for wholeness of spirit, and wholeness of spirit means a harmonious, dynamic interplay of the qualities of spirit with the qualities of soul taking place through the body, with a community of others, in the world. We will describe the contribution of a psychology of integration to this quest.

When thinking, feeling, and willing are transformed by being brought into connection with the higher-ego, thinking becomes truth, feeling becomes beauty, and willing becomes goodness. Truth, beauty, and goodness may seem to us to be Platonic abstractions; they are not abstract, but have been lost for so long that we have forgotten the experience and remember only the names, or, at most, we have only philosophical conceptions of these virtues.

When the higher-ego, or self, is stirred, the lower-ego, the worldly 'I', diminishes; it is no longer the center of importance. This relativizing
of the lower-ego, its movement off center stage is felt as loneliness, depression, anxiety and fear. A psychotherapist must learn to recognize the difference between neurotic isolation, loneliness, and depression and the quite healthy deflation of the dominating worldly 'I'.

The qualitative difference is found in the realm of feeling. Neurotic isolation, depression and anxiety is accompanied by feelings of anger and rage that are not expressed or are expressed in veiled complaints against others and thus involve an imbalance among thinking, feeling, and willing. The lower-ego is not functioning harmoniously.

When a person is experiencing the displacement of the lower-ego from the center, there is a felt need to spend much more time alone, which must be distinguished from loneliness. Depression does occur, but without feelings of hatred or attempts to accuse anyone else of causing the feeling one experienced; there is much more a sense that things that used to work in one's life no longer work. And there is actually an element of relief in this kind of depression. Anxiety and fear have a rather 'sweet' quality, though I am not using the term 'sweet' as saying the experience is enjoyable. The difference between the neurotic form of this condition and the healthy form is the former is felt is felt as an absolute threat while the latter

is felt as life threatening but necessary, though the meaning is unclear. The healthy displacement of the worldly 'I' signals the possibility of true transformation, a re-birth of thinking, feeling and willing into a new place of existence.

I have described, from the viewpoint of a psychology of integration, a necessary task of psychology – the bringing into harmony of thinking, feeling, and willing. As long as thinking, feeling, and willing are at odds, transformation is not possible. So, a lot of the work of spiritual psychology is oriented toward encouraging this harmony, and it is quite amazing to see this going on in therapy once you know how to see from within. Let us go through one more story concerning psychotherapy operating at this level in order to stay close to the inner sense of this work; then we can go on to describe the integrated psychology of transformation.

Recently, a middle aged man, very bright, a geologist, entered therapy because it seemed that his relationship with his wife was about to fall apart. After several sessions, that difficulty seemed to abate, but he then said that he wanted to leave his job. He said that he was full of fear that he did not have the ability required to carry out a very large project that would require concentrated effort over the next five years. The task is indeed large, and he does not seem to have the support from his employer to do this task effectively. However, what most interested me was the feeling of fear, for it seemed to be the same feeling that he described when he was having difficulty in his relationship.

When we experience fear, we want to get away from it and

usually cannot see that fear is a primary way our feeling life gets our attention. The patient told two dreams during one session that address this issue of fear. In the first dream, the dreamer was checking on one of his colleagues who was in charge of inspecting a plant to make sure it followed the standards of environmental control. As he approached the plant, the colleague was driving a large truck out of the plant with a load of sludge. The dreamer stopped his colleague and asked him what he was doing. The colleague said that when he inspected the plant, it was perfectly clean except for this one pile of mess. Rather than make a detailed report on this violation, he decided to carry it off and dump it.

The dream provides an entry into the patient's fear. He is afraid that he needs to know to make things run right. There is much more to the dream, but I want to emphasize this fear of loosing control. And this fear of losing control, while stimulated by the situation of his job, is the same fear that entered into his relationship with
his wife. He feared that he would lose control of her. When he felt that fear he wanted to leave his marriage, when he felt the same fear at work he wanted to quit his job. To concentrate on his marriage or on his job, however, would be to miss what the soul is trying to present, the experience of fear. And the important task for this patient is to learn to enter into fear. When this unpleasant feeling enters, he tends to seek ways to further control and to further deny fear. The fear is not caused by his wife or his job; it is his repressed feeling life.

The second dream gets closer to the fear. In this dream, the dreamer is on a train in Africa. An old woman on the train is selling toy monsters, but is afraid she cannot get anyone interested in them. Then suddenly, the toy monsters are large, live monsters, pursuing the train. The train speeds up to escape the monsters, but as it does so, sparks fly from the engine and catch the train on fire.

Here, it becomes more apparent that the patient's fears do not have to do with the possibility that his wife may leave or that he may not be capable of doing the job he is required, but that the fears are within himself, feelings that he has treated as toys when presented to him by his soul. Now these feelings are alive and appear as unknown animal creatures. When the head attempts to escape from what the soul presents, the speeding up to leave the feelings behind results in burn out.

The high mental capacity of this patient enables him to run away from his feelings. His task is to relinquish attempting to control through his mind, stay with and in the fear, and give attention to the developing of relationship. In working at this task, a harmony will develop among thinking, feeling, and willing.

Harmony among thinking, feeling, and willing is needed in order to enter into the task of a more complete integration. This integration concerns the development of capacities to experience thought, feeling, and willing as not belonging exclusively to oneself, but as the very qualities of the world. Integration concerns the development of full participation in the spiritual nature of the world; it is the complete dynamic intermingling of the subjective and the objective. Psychotherapy suffers severe limitations if it does not encourage the ability to be in the world differently, which requires experiencing the world in a way that does not separate us from it as onlookers. We do not as yet have a therapy that is able to make the bridge between the individual and the world. When such a therapy develops, it can be a true world-shaping force. As it is now, we work with patients on their own issues and problems and then send them back out into a sick world. Hopefully with sufficient strength to endure it. We hope that politics or economics or religion or art or science or technology will produce the world changes that bring health. But none of these approaches alone or all together will produce the necessary changes. We must be in the world differently for the world to be different.

The particular quality of experience in which thought is no longer subjective but has an objective quality, we can call imagination. Imagination is typically understood to be a subjective experience, but such a designation characterizes confusion between fantasy and imagination. Any artist knows in a very immediate way, with absolute certainty, that imagination is objective and subjective at the same time. If we take guidance from the artist and can begin to understand psychology not so much as a science, but living psychology as an art of life, then we can understand how imagination is a transformation of thought. What first strikes us in forming this relation between thought and imagination is how what we ordinarily call thought is not at all creative, but in fact is nothing more than memory. Ordinarily, our thoughts are not living thinking, but dead thinking. We constantly utilize already completed thoughts, which are memory, with which to think, and such dead thinking becomes functional through the use of logic. Great cleverness and invention are worlds away from imagination. In order for intellectual logic to function, thought must be kept apart from feeling and willing. In spite of the fact that, in a certain sense, present culture respects and elevates dead thinking, and even institutionalizes it into universities, this kind of thinking is on the side of death rather than on the side of life and constitutes a psychological disorder of culture.

When psychotherapy proceeds along the path we have been pursuing, in which thinking, feeling, and willing are, through the patient's efforts brought into harmony, these three dimensions of experience come to a state of readiness for radical transformation. The dynamic flow among thinking, feeling, and willing produces a change in thinking. Thinking is no longer separated from feeling and willing. Thinking becomes imbued, interpenetrated, with feeling and willing. Thinking becomes whole. And because thinking becomes whole, it has a life of its own. Thought comes to life when it is a whole being. The dynamic confluence of thinking, feeling, and willing at the pole of thinking, what I call imagination, comes to life, however, only when the grasping quality of the lower-ego yields to a receiving quality from the higher-ego, when the ego-self becomes spirit-self. The creative action of imagination does not originate from the

46

subjectivity of thought, but from the unity of self and spirit.

In psychotherapy, much can be done in the interaction between patient and therapist to encourage harmonizing thought (the shadow of spirit), feeling the shadow of heart-presence), and willing (the shadow of true embodiment-as-experience). The transformation of thought into imagination, because it is founded upon the absolute freedom of the individual to open and be receptive to spirit, seems to be much more a matter of grace.

When thought relinquishes its grasping mode and is infused with feeling and willing, the patients will go through a time of confusion, a kind of breakdown which is actually a breakthrough, the controlling character of dead thought and logic no longer works, and the sharp division between ourselves and the outer world, which is maintained by the onlooker perspective of thought dissolves, and the two dark companions of dead thought, judgment and isolation, lose their power. The confusion of the patient during this time is quite great; patients who are particularly mental go through the most, for, usually, people with higher mental ability have learned to utilize intelligence as the way to remain removed from feeling and
willing, and have counted at the same time on their intelligence to survive. Thus, for a time, their survival may seem threatened. At the same time, the infusion of feeling and willing into thought brings about a forgotten vitality. So the patient is placed into a situation of true, free choice, a choice that is not an intellectual operation of weighing sides, looking at all the angles and then moving in a way judgment seem to point, but an opportunity to freely say, 'yes' to spirit.

What has thus far been described as the transformation of thought into imagination concerns not only patients in psychotherapy. Therapists seldom advance to this level themselves because it is typically not an aspect of their own education. Psychology is taught as an intellectual discipline, and even when feeling or willing is addressed, it is from an onlooker perspective. If a patient advances from the level of harmoniously connecting thought, feeling, and willing to a point of integration, a therapist is likely to understand the time of confusion the patient goes through as a regression, or, the movement of therapy will come to a standstill and therapy will end. Because there is the likelihood that therapy currently ends at the edge of spirit, integration is never addressed.

To remedy this situation, the self-education of

 the therapist must be an ongoing matter. The great psychologists such as Jung, Freud, and Adler fully understood this necessity; even more so is this self-education a need for a spiritual psychology of integration. The manner in which this self-awareness can take place that is suitable for the situation of a psychology of integration is through meditation. However, such a meditation practice comes out of the view of human reality we have thus far presented, and is not borrowed from the Eastern paths.

Our thought images are characterized by being but shadows of the direct perception of an object. The difference between a thought image of a pencil and the direct sensory awareness of that pencil is vast. The shadowy character of the thought-image leads us to consider thought subjective. Through concentrated meditation on a thought-image in which the whole personality, in its thought, feeling, and willing is completely centered on the object, the thought-image gradually becomes as vivid as the direct sense perception. This meditation, carried out five minutes each day, awakens the power of imagination. Such a meditation appears quite easy; it is not. Nevertheless, it strikes me as quite amazing that people will spend years of their life practicing forms of yoga breathing and contortions of the body, or will work with great intensity to focus on nothing, but would look at the meditation required to awaken imagination as trivial. Certainly, if spirit remains asleep in therapists it will remain asleep in patients, or if it awakens will be scared away by the therapist.

The transformation of thought into imagination, in which the higher-ego finds connection to the lower-ego, results in the capacity to stand in truth. Truth is both subjective and objective at the same time. The traditional definition of truth is the conformity of the mind with the object. We understand this definition as two separate entities coming together, when actually, truth is the dynamic field of reality, given in image-form, in which the polarity of spirit and ego perception of the world live in harmonious balance. Truth is neither subjective nor objective, but the capacity, through spirit, to perceive spirit in the world. Imagination, we could say, consists of the spiritual perception of the things of the world.

At the same time a transformation from thought to imagination takes place, another movement from lower-ego to higher-ego also occurs. The life of feeling, even when in harmony with thinking and willing is taken to be something quite subjective. However, when feeling becomes interpenetrated with thought and will, a state of readiness exists for feeling to find a new center, the heart. A vast difference exists between ego feelings and heart feeling. This difference concerns the birth of the spirit in the heart, which changes the subjectivity of feeling into the impulse to share oneself with others, the impulse of brotherhood, of community.

As thinking transforms into imagination and the objectivity of spirit is read in the world, the interpenetration of feeling with thought moves our thinking from the region of the head to the region of the heart. Similarly, the interpenetration of feeling with willing moves our actions from impulsiveness and reaction to the responsiveness of serving.

Feelings, in the usual, subjective sense, are intimately interwoven with our ego-identification with the world. We usually connect feelings with someone or some event in the world as if those feelings are a result of actions of some other person or some situation. Thus, the objectivity of feelings goes unrecognized. The self-education of the therapist can be furthered immeasurably through a specifically Western form of

meditation that brings to light the autonomous character of feeling. The meditation consists of remembering a person or an event in which one experienced a particular feeling, comfortable or uncomfortable. The past scene must be re-created in memory in vivid image form, with all the details of the occurrence, so that there is a re-living of the feeling from the inside and not just an outside
memory of the event. When vividly established in memory with all of its feelings, the scene is then extinguished and what is held within are the feelings, now freed from the particular person or situation in which they occurred. The autonomy of feelings can then begin to be a real experience, and either blaming others or situations for our feelings drops away as the soul, through this meditation practice, strengthens so that it is no longer dependent on setting up outer situations in order to try to draw our attention to its own dynamic qualities.

As we begin to experience the autonomous movement of the soul in feeling, we experience more of the great mystery of the soul. What (this 'what' is actually a 'who'), within the soul itself is the reason for its movement? It is love within the soul that is the reason for its movement. Feeling is the inner dynamism of the spirit in the soul telling us that we are here to grow and to change and to find connection to our soul. Feeling tells us that our soul has an inner guide, that change and movement is not random. This, we can feel as we learn to feel from within the region of the heart.

In the Grail story, the *Parsifal* of Wolfram von Eschenbach, one of the most significant adventures concerns the movement into the feelings of the heart. This adventure involves Gawain rather than Parsifal, for in this epic,
Parsifal represents the transformation of thought into imagination and Gawain represents the transformation of ego feelings into feelings of the heart. Gawain is required to go to the castle of dark magic and undergo a trial. The trial consists of spending a night in a room in the castle, a room that has a magic bed. The bed has rollers on it, and the floor is made of red ruby. As soon as one jumps onto the bed, it begins to whirl around violently in ceaseless motion. Gawain jumps onto the

bed and is thrown around the room, hanging on for dear life. He does well with the task, but after a long ordeal at this, a huge, ferocious lion enters the room, and he does battle with it. Gawain cut off one of its legs, but it continues to attack him; finally, he kills the lion. Gawain nearly dies in the process of this ordeal. Here, we have an image of entering into the life of feeling, and we can recognize that this task is most difficult. To enter fully into our feelings, to stop blaming others for what we feel and to stop blaming situations for what we feel, throws us into the violent motion of feeling. I bring us this image in order to point out that the meditation previously described is a difficult task indeed, for there are very disturbing forces in the dynamics of the soul, and great courage is needed to stay within feeling, but, in the very center of feeling life, the soul finds peace in the region of the heart.

Many therapies emphasize the importance of feelings. For the most part, the object of such therapies is to encourage patients to find connection with their feelings and to bring feeling into harmony with thinking and willing. But, the object of a psychology of integration is to encourage movement from the lower-ego to the higher-ego, and in the sphere of feeling this means to find the center of feeling in the heart. We want to feel and at the same time we want to defend our feelings, to get them to work the way we think they should work. Getting to the heart of feeling requires yielding to the divine source within our soul.

I am reminded of a patient whose work in therapy clearly centers on the quest for the heart. She is a woman who, during the sixties was very involved in the peace movement, a real flower child. Indeed, that time was a time when feeling predominated as a movement within our culture, but did not gather the inner strength to produce significant change. We can recognize that time, though, as centering in feeling, a search for a higher level of feeling, because it focused on attempts to establish a real community of feeling. Like Gawain's fight with the lion, there were many feeling forces of a dark nature, the chief one at that time being drugs. And this woman, at that time, was conquered by the lion. She became deeply involved in drugs of every sort, finally concluding with heroin.

Nevertheless, she continued the fight, and conquered that attack of dark feeling forces; she went on to become a Montessori teacher, clearly a choice to follow a life of service to others. So, here, we can see how staying with feelings, entering them, fighting the swirl of forces, produces a transformation of personal feeling from a 'me' consciousness to a 'we' consciousness. She is still on the path to the center of feeling in the heart.

Recently, this patient was talking about her struggle to come to experience the difference between voluntary service and involuntary service. By this, she meant that it is hard for her to tell when she is doing things for others because others ask her to and when she is serving others out of the deepest feeling of her heart. She told this dream: In the dream, she is out in nature, hiking on a path, and un-trodden path up the side of a mountain. The dreamer is with another woman, a friend. There are some men working on the path, making a small way. The dreamer looks down and notices that she has no shoes on, and, with her friend, has to turn around and go back to get her shoes. At the bottom of the path, when she returns to the starting place, she finds that her car is stuck in the mud. She and her friend place something under the wheels of the car, and it is then able to move.

The dream is a dream of movement, a journey along a path, a journey upward, like the movement of feeling from the level of the lower-ego to the level of the higher-ego. But she is making her way on this path in a kind of natural state. She is not sufficiently conscious of he fact that she is on a spiritual journey. She has to go back and get the equipment that will aid her on this path. The friend of the dreamer in the dream is, in the waking life of the dreamer someone who the dreamer recognizes as a very spiritual person. In Jungian terms, we would see this figure in the dream as a shadow figure, that part of the dreamer, which the dreamer is not fully aware of.

The friend is the spirit guide of the dreamer's soul.

The dreamer's journey back down the path to retrieve her shoes and to get the car moving, indicate that the dreamer has undertaken the path without being sufficiently grounded in the physical world. Like her early years, there is a tendency on the part of the dreamer to split the lower-ego from the higher-ego, and attempt to follow the path of the higher-ego without taking the worldly concerns of the lower-ego into account. As she learns to do this, her feeling life will become more substantial, more real. She can then find the feeling center of her heart.

As the transformation of thought into imagination leads to standing in truth, the transformation of feeling to heart leads to beauty. Beauty also is neither subjective nor objective, but simultaneously subjective and objective, the apprehension of the soul in all things. Beauty does not mean beautifying, adornments, decorations, nor does it mean task or aesthetics. Beauty means the perception of the heart, the unifying of the center of one's being with the center of being in all its manifestations. As a refinement, not in an effete sense, but as finding the center of being, beauty is the manifestation of the divine in the world, in all appearances. All things, as they display their inner nature, present beauty. Beauty is not an attribute of things, but the essence of things given in sensate form, the divine touching the senses. Through beauty, the particularity of each thing shows forth and is honored and we are brought into intimacy with the specific variety of each individual, each thing in the world. Through beauty, the world is taken to heart.

The third transformation concerns the will. We must keep in mind that the will is not a mental faculty, but is actually connected with the most physical aspect of our being, the metabolism and the muscles. Will is the most unconscious aspect of the soul, concerned with the animation of the body, making the human body more than a conglomeration of physiology.
While, from the viewpoint of ordinary perception, the sphere

of will, once understood as interwoven with the physical body rather than being a mental faculty, is the lowest part of our being, from the viewpoint of the higher-ego, will is the highest aspect of our being. The development of the will, its transformation from the lower to the higher-ego, brings about the actuality of freedom, manifested as goodness. The difficulty in development of the will can be seen in all of our habits. With habits we experience the binding of freedom to the body. When thinking and feeling are in harmonious relation with willing, then thinking and feeling begin to interpenetrate into the sphere of the will. This infusion of thought and feeling into will is experienced as wishing and longing. Thus, the dimension of will ranges from habit or desire, where we are least free, through wishing, which is more free, but transient, to longing, which is more enduring, but still bound.

The transformation of will involves a significant alteration of all three of these aspects. Freedom of will consists of a total merging of the lower-ego with the higher-ego. No therapy can bring about this level of development. The task involves no less than entering fully into the immediate experience of all levels of our being – instinct, drives, desires, sense, dreams, thoughts, actions, memories, fantasies, as these occur at the level of the lower self, and sacrificing, that is, giving all this over to the higher self. The development of pure willing involves a life of total self-sacrifice. The difficult task of self-sacrifice lies in the fact that it involves the denial of nothing, but the full realization of everything, most importantly the realization that the darkest sides of our selves, that which we most forcefully deny, must be embraced as a brother or sister. Even approaching such a level of development is not possible without having gone through the transformation of thought into imagination and feeling into heart. The appeal of self-sacrifice is filled with illusions. Religion appeals to the longing for self-sacrifice, but often does not provide an understanding of what is actually involved and confuses self-sacrifice with denial of vast portions of our being. Such idealism produces much damage.

Conclusion

The goals of a spiritual psychology, a psychology of full and true integration, are, first, to explore and develop the new picture consciousness that can bring about connection again to the ancient wisdom of spiritual reality. This aspect of integration gives validity to the experience of soul and the capacity to strengthen the soul forces. The purpose of psychotherapy is thus changed from adjustment to the development of the soul. Second, the aim of integration is to bring about a freeing of the
blockage among thinking, feeling and willing that produce so much damage in the individual life. This freeing of the functioning of the soul is accompanied by a new appreciation of the body and the recognition of the polar character of the I, a realization that spirit in our culture must engage in worldly tasks while at the same time quest for true freedom of spirit. Third, the aim of integration is to be in the world differently and contribute to the making of a different world – a world that can be sensed, perceived, creatively engaged through soul, spirit, and heart, felt as permeated with spirit. In this world we develop the capacity to stand in the truth of imagination, perceiving soul in all things, feel the soul in the particulars of the world in heart-centered beauty, and seek goodness in a unity of spirit-life, work-life, and social life. Goodness is seeking the wholeness of others, in the formation of community. The psychology of integration, founded in soul, developed through spirit, and brought into the world is the necessary counter-force to the impending illusions of mastering the world through science and technology and the illusion of conquering the necessary 'craziness' that prompts movement toward wholeness through therapies that are concerned with adjustment rather than transformation or utilize drugs to obscure what motivates soul movement.

Addendum

The Dimensions of Therapeutic Awareness

An Introduction to Spiritual Therapeutic

This paper appeared in the British journal, *Self and Society: The International Journal of Humanistic Psychology*

Human beings, along with Earth and Her creatures, are undergoing vast and deep and permanent alterations as well as extinctions. Such transmutations, due to technological developments in all fields, accompanied with cultural degradations of soul and spirit life, are aspects of humanity's taking over, completely, who we are and who we will become, but doing so, mainly, with very little self-knowledge.

If transmutation occurs without being met with deep inner awareness, unsustainability of Earth's natural bounty and destruction of the very nature of being human are the inevitable result. Any consideration of therapeutics, within every realm of practice, must take into account this context. Doing so, even with a minimum of contemplation, reveals that along with the given
therapeutic applications of the wisdom of the Spiritual Science of Rudolf Steiner, 'therapeutic living' becomes a necessity. Body, soul, spirit – willing, feeling, thinking, now require therapeutic nurturing as a way of life, a nurturing of 'innerness', in a time when the very notion of the importance and significance of an inner life is becoming obscure.

I have taken up this task of developing ways of therapeutic living for some thirty years, together with Cheryl Sanders-Sardello, until her recent death, under the rubric of 'Spiritual Psychology'. This psychology was never intended to be 'anthroposophical psychology', another psychology, existing alongside probably hundreds of other approaches to psychology, to be utilized mainly by anthroposophists. I have taken up this task, not as an anthroposophist, but as an anthroposopher, as one deeply dedicated to Anthroposophy, but unconstrained by what is deemed acceptable and 'orthodox'.

Not only am I an anthoposopher, I am an anthroposopher of Rudolf Steiner's 'alternate way'. In *Occult Science, An Outline*, he speaks of his way of Anthroposophy as "the direct path of knowledge". He speaks of another possible path of Anthroposophy, "The path of 'feeling'":

"The path of feeling, however, turns directly to feeling only and seeks to ascend from this to knowledge. It is based on the fact that when the soul surrenders itself completely to a feeling for a certain length of time, this feeling transforms itself into knowledge, into a picture like perception. If, for example, the soul fills itself completely during weeks, months, or even a longer period, with the feeling of humility, then the content of feeling transforms itself into a perception. One may, by passing step by step through such feelings, also find a path into the super-sensible regions. "(Occult Science 2pg.379)

Rudolf Steiner goes on to say that the path of feeling is not very suitable for this time because it requires that one have a great deal of solitude in life in order to carry out the contemplations needed to go through this form of soul development. I have solved this difficulty, though, with my researches into silence, given in *Silence: The Mystery of Wholeness*. There, suitable ways are presented on being within the Silence in the midst of our wild and chaotically busy world. Once Silence is felt as an actual presence, a being rather than a 'state achieved', we have the necessary inner guidance for deepening into the Silence in the midst of any condition whatsoever.

I have developed multiple ways of following the 'Path of Feeling". Immersing oneself in each of these 'steps' opens the possibility of therapeutic living.

Attention

The capacity of attention, when opened as experience, attentiveness, dissolves the distinction between 'inner' and 'outer' that characterizes ordinary consciousness. Non-duality characterizes the consciousness that is attention. If I say, "pay attention", doing so requires using attention while not being within it. "I" feel as if I am here, a kind of onlooker, who then notices something over there, separate from the attention. Attention, as a capacity, is always attention within attention, and what is tended is never 'on its own'. It is immersed and nurtured within spirit, now awakened.

Attention is the mysterious place of our true freedom. When we are within our attention, nothing can confine it. When we are not within our attention, however, it is subject to being captured every moment by external activity manipulate desires. Without the capacity of attention, we live in constant nervousness.

The Silence
There is a strong tendency to imagine silence as the absence of sound, as merely being quiet. Such a way of imagining silence deprives it of being anything in itself. The Silence exists everywhere, around us, and within everything in the world, expressing differently wherever noticed. For example, the silence of a brook forms one 'tone' of the Silence, while the Silence
of a grove of trees forms another, while the Silence within the noisiness of streets sounds of a city yet another; are all one Silence of many manifestations. Silence never goes away. We go away from it. It is the 'other side' of existence, the 'in' of ex-istence. Silence is like the 'container' of all contents, and when a content is understood without noticing the Silence, content limits itself to being only information, often acting as if it is knowledge. With the felt presence of the Silence, everything is being born each instant.

Silence is wholly receptive, so we notice it only when we are open and receptive, radically so. Then, the presence of the

Silence becomes palpable. Being able to feel the objective presence of Silence has great soul value. Silence initiates peace within the life of the soul. Silence mediates the polarities of soul life. Without presence to silence, the polarities of soul life are experienced as in conflict and full of contradiction.

The substance of silence stands between the contradictions and contraries of soul life and prevents them from fighting each other. The contradictions meet, not head on and directly, but have to travel through the medium of silence, which graces each of the contradictions.

Silence is the medium of therapeutic healing because spirit re-creates us through the medium of silence. Without the substance of silence we cannot free ourselves from all that has affected us from the past.

Heart Awareness
Heart-awareness, heartfulness, locates the experience of being human within the soul and spiritual center of the body, the heart. Here, soul and spirit unite within body, assuring we are not only biology and physiology, but are of the 'middle world'.

The practice of heartfulness contemplatively engages the actual organ of the heart, inwardly revealing what it is like to be incarnated as body and in the

In developing the capacity to creatively radiate from the center outward, the holy, whole, nature of the human body reveals itself as intimately united with imagination, creative presence, and the earthly world.

Heartfulness feels like our natural state, forgotten, long ago.

Heartfulness, the 'middle place' between thinking and willing, originates non-dual presence in everyday life, existing between ourselves and everything visible and invisible, given as the most primary way of know as 'being-with', that is, intimate, intuitive knowing.

By becoming what we are present with, through the rhythm of body, intensified most completely within the heart, we know by communion rather than by the distance of mental-ness.

Heartfulness can be lived and experienced, not just in moments of the practice of contemplation, but as sensing, perceiving, knowing, and non-causal action.

Heartfulness alters what we know as power, into receptive-action, in harmony with the rhythms of Earth and Cosmos, from our feet to our head, from the widest expanses to the deepest interior.

Death Awareness

Death-awareness differs, infinitely, from 'awareness-of-death'. Death-awareness precedes awareness of death, though it is not conscious unless held in contemplation, within the Silence, and Attention.

The Whole of Life consists of that 'half' we call living and that half we speak of as death. The two are always the fullness of Life, something different than the 'content' of living. We have lost that sense of wholeness. An interval, time, exists in ordinary consciousness between life and death. This makes death seem across that border, and makes death seem repugnant. Contemplated deeply, the temporal demarcation between 'living' and 'death dissolves into Life.

Living is the specific content of Life, the daily unfolding in particulars, while Life is the container. We are always within the 'container', the infinite 'now' and within that container, there is no death. The body dies, but "I" do not die.

Once this truth is experienced in contemplation, it also opens us to being present, in feeling, which is nonetheless very specific, with anyone whose body has died. This expanded presence leads to experiencing everything that occurs in our earthly being as an intimate composing of the relation of the living and those whose body has died. Fear of dying dissolves, never completely, but we are no longer subject to the dominance of anxiety.

Language Awareness

Language is given to us. It exists before we begin to speak. The gift is beyond all experience, yet exists for us. Words are related to the eternal word. When emptied of this dimension, they first become knowledge, then mere information, and then empty, and we waste away. Very few words of fullness of Being are left, and contemplatively entering those words can lead us away from merely using language into offering our speaking-being as the medium of presence of spiritual reality. Among these special, still living words are: Love, Death, Wonder, Life, and a few others.

Self-Awareness

The riddle of the "I". The "I" is the beginning and the end, the ultimate truth. Distinctions are made between the 'lower self" and the 'higher self". Or the 'I' is sometimes spoken of as 'the Christ in me'. But, what is the experience like?

We cannot add anything to our Being to become self-aware. Rather, everything has to be taken away of what we think we know of ourselves, and even what we are. Self-Awareness is 'no-thing'. It cannot be thought, it cannot be felt, and it cannot be willed. To try and 'grasp' the "I", the "I" had to become separate from itself. Thus, we take "I" to be the related to the 'me'. And, similarly, think that, somehow, it is possible to get from the 'me' to the 'I".

Self-Awareness can be experienced only within and as utter Stillness, something radically deeper than the Silence. It is pure receptivity, radical receptivity. Spiritual traditions have always known this and provide elaborate ways of stripping personality. These ways, though, often take one into a tradition, a religion, a "Way", where the simplicity of self-awareness can easily yield to particular surrounds deemed necessary for its realization.

Within the I, there is only listening. The I listens, that is all, and everything. Within the poise of listening, tremendous activity occurs. We are still, and the I speaks through us, through the senses. This brings about a fundamental change in which there Is no 'positive' activity, no 'self-expression'. Surrender is the way. Within the I, everything is present, it is not leaving this world for the spiritual worlds, but everything is no-thing and no-thing is everything, and yet specific and revealed through sensing.

Sense Awareness

I cannot use the phrase 'sensory awareness here" because that phrase is now commonly understood as meaning intensified presence to the sensory world through the various senses. Within an awakened "I", however, what can be immediately experienced is that the senses are not within us, we are within the senses.

Think of sensing as the act of the "I" giving itself to the world. Sensation is not the result of the stimulation of the sense organs, which are only media of transmission. Sensation is the non-dual receptivity of soul. If I can sense what someone else is sensing, then the senses are not inside the body. To call such sensing empathy, is only to name a phenomenon, and, typically, to go on and make a theory or that phenomenon, like the theory of empathy, rather than tending what actually happens. To be present within the act of sensing in this manner requires developing the intuitive capacities of the heart, gradually feeling them spread through the body, where sensing unites into whole presence.

We are soul- sensitive to sensory impressions, not through the sensory organs, that is a secondary matter, but through the medium of the senses. This medium fills all space and contains all sight, smell, sound, and the rest of the senses. All the senses are variations of light and light contains all the elements of the senses. The I is the fount of sensing, or the light. This light can vary in strength, and thus sensing canbe expanded or contracted. We identify sensing with a contraction of light into physical form. Clairvoyance, though, is the instance of expanded sensing into clear sensing, whether that be seeing, or hearing, or touch, or any of the senses.

Spiritual-Earth Awareness

Before I-awareness began to emerge, millennia ago, human consciousness and Earth consciousness were the same. The vestiges of that consciousness occur in moments of feeling the exquisite joy, calmness, wonder, that occur within the natural world. Such consciousness can become the opening into the possibility of spiritual-earth awareness. This mode of awareness is critical to therapeutic presence of any kind, for any therapeutic activity occurring within wholeness is also Earth-healing and world healing.

Besides the three states of waking, sleeping, and dreaming, there is a state that is even deeper, the embrace of Earth. We experience only vestiges of it, when we sometimes awaken with a sweet feeling, deep and throughout the body.

Touching into the embrace of Earth, the overwhelming sense is that Earth lives wholly within joy, is wholly receptive, and Earth as we see and feel and experience Earth, when fully present, is the outward expression of this joy.

This state of Earth-embrace can also be approached in very deep contemplation, starting with being within the deepest of Silence, utter Stillness. Then, from within the Stillness, if the lips gesture the word 'Earth" (within the Stillness, word and the content of the word are one activity), the whole of Stillness reconfigures into the sweet embrace of Earth, a state that can now be sustained within contemplative awareness. From there, it becomes possible to be contemplatively within any dimension of Earth.

For example, if, from within the presence of the sweet Earth, the word 'Tree" is gestured, the whole of one's being enters being 'tree'.

Within Earth-consciousness trees are inwardly present and experienced, with immediacy, as Earth's individuating awareness, something like the "I" of Earth. The sap of trees, from within tree-sensation, is felt as an incredible flow of strength, the strength of the inner earth reaching

to unite with sky, full of strength, something experienced like 'joy-strength-awareness'. Trees awareness as something like beings who live Earth awareness, each, and One at the same time, root and sky as one, all as perfect Silence and Stillness, a single tree, all trees, Whole Earth-awareness.

Rudolf Steiner's "Second Way", the way of feeling, takes one into the depths of the Spiritual
Earth, which is the ground, for us, for any therapeutic act. If we go deep enough, we find ourselves as if facing, meeting Rudolf Steiner, in the region of knowledge.

****

These eight ways do not complete the description of therapeutic awareness. There are others, such as 'relating', 'conversation', 'healing', 'Stillness', 'virtue'. Nor are the ones introduced here sufficiently detailed, though they are spoken in such a manner that the truth
of them can be felt, while not confined to the manner spoken here.

How does one then enter this ground of inherent therapeutic presence? What is spoken here is from the realm of Wisdom. Not 'my' wisdom, but what occurs through inner listening. It cannot be taught, not as anything of a 'positivistic' nature, not as a set of skills to add on to who we are. There is nothing to learn, for learning would make what is immediate seem both distant and mental.

We develop into the ground of therapeutic awareness through a process of removal, of
subtraction rather than addition. Each of these eight ways of therapeutic awareness, for example, begin to be noticed by subtracting the
overlays of personality, acquired knowledge, power, identity, prestige, position, and most of all, spiritual greed.

This manner of developing therapeutic awareness is not

however a variation of the 'via negativa' of mysticism. The realm of Wisdom can become science, and science here is practical wisdom. Feeling lives within Wisdom, and Wisdom is experienced as radical receptivity.

Robert Sardello offers guided development of all of the dimensions of Therapeutic Awareness outlined here, in the form of one on one meetings, by phone or by Skype, for twelve weeks, a two hour session each week.

This therapeutic training is not only for therapists, counselors, and spiritual directors, but for anyway seeking to develop the capacities that are detailed in this book.

The details and costs are available either on the website: www.robertsardello.com or by emailing me directly: spiritualheart@heartfulsoul.com

Made in the USA
San Bernardino, CA
22 April 2018